tarot flip

Marcus Katz & Tali Goodwin

Cover: 'Queen of Cups', Tyldwick Tarot © by Neil Lovell

http://www.malpertuis.co.uk/tyldwick/

KDP Edition

Published by Forge Press (2020)

1 Wood Cottage, Old Windebrowe, Keswick, Cumbria CA12 4NT

This Tarosophy® Kickstart Reference Book is dedicated to those who provided original material for this work, in particular:

TaliTarot, Mary, LionTamer76, Mystickal Skyies, Tinkerbell, Kevin, Deborah, Liz, Polgara, Rootweaver, Mercurian, Sweet Stacey Rose, Taldaanja, Spike, SandigoMandi, Aurora Wiseheart, Dee, Isabel, TrueTarot, Andraxas, Pearl, Donnaleigh, Lua Astrology, Kimmie, Peaceful Panther, Heavenly7073, Shannon, Karebear … and all the Citizens & Patrons of Tarot Town.

Find us in discussion with more than 35,000 Tarot Students, Readers and Teachers for the best in innovative Tarot in our Facebook group **Tarot Professionals** and enjoy the membership benefits of the Tarot Association at **www.tarotassociation.net**.

Tarosophy® is a registered trademark.

CONTENTS

*The Essential Workbook inspired by Tarot Readers **for** Tarot Readers!*

Introduction

In this exclusive and innovative Tarosophy® teaching, you will discover the actual meanings of the Tarot cards as they have come to be seen by a range of experienced Tarot Readers. These meanings have been gathered from hundreds of Tarot Readers throughout our social media platforms and then collated and reviewed to provide an essential quick-start reference guide for new and experienced readers alike.

These are not just the keywords and themes that a book will tell you, but the actual unconscious ideas that an experienced Tarot reader is accessing when they look at these cards in readings. You may be surprised by how obvious or surprising some of these concepts are when comparing them to book meanings. Over time a Tarot card reader comes to see the cards in many contexts and therefore deepens their experience of each card.

These meanings have been generated by using NLP (Neuro-Linguistic Programming) and language patterns to ask questions of experienced Tarot card readers in such a way as to be able to generate the unconscious processes and field of thought that underpin the responses. Combined with the experience of reading for over 10,000 people and books such as the *Definitive Tarot* by Bill Butler (called *The Tarot Bible* in some countries) we have collated this list as an essential reference, particularly for beginners looking for a 'simple answer' for each card in their first few readings.

These meanings have also been derived from many different decks; both classic and contemporary, ensuring a wide range of interpretations have been applied.

You can now short-cut years of book learning to start with the experience of hundreds of readers!

We have organized this reference book into the four suits of Pentacles, Cups, Swords and Wands. We have then provided an entry for each of the cards running through that suit, from Ace to Ten and then the Court Cards of Page, Knight, Queen and King. We have given a reference guide to the 22 Major Cards at the end of this book.

For each suit and card, we have assigned a new title, drawn from the summary of all the entries we received for the cards. It became apparent, for example, that experienced readers see the Pentacles as "being about" resource – in all its forms, whether material, physical, health, career, etc.

When asked what the cards were NOT, most readers – when we compiled the answers – saw the Aces as not being 'endings' (and therefore we refer to them upright as 'seeds') and the Twos of every suit as being disorganized – hence we give them the upright title of Organization.

In some cases, we "flipped" between synonyms and antonyms, exploring the various descriptions offered by readers until we settled on a final single keyword. This is why this title is called *Tarot Flip*!

This then allows us to title each card, such as the TWO of PENTACLES being titled "The Organization of Resources". These general yet innovative and contemporary titles may also provide you insight into applying the card in any position in any spread in response to any question. They have been generated through the experience of hundreds of Tarot readers, distilled from their original learning in books via long-term application and experience.

For each card we have provided a keyword or concept, for both the upright and flipped meaning. We have then also suggested – and these are merely suggestions – what you might actually say to phrase these words in delivering an interpretation of the card. This will always depend on the position and context of the card, although the phrases here are a kickstart.

We have provided as many different ways of talking about the cards as possible – in fact, 78 different ways – to give you a flavor of how experienced Tarot card readers might phrase their interpretation. However, it is most important that you use this as a kickstart only and learn to discover your own unique voice through the Tarot!

To further assist your readings, we have given a "thematic attractor" for each card, or "frame". This is the basic unconscious building-block of the card – the main field or value in which the meanings of the card are generated.

So for example, one card may be all about "possession" whilst its keywords all fall into that general idea, such as 'donating', 'giving', 'saving' etc. By contemplating this frame you will discover many ways of applying the card to the variety of questions you will be asked. The second Tarosophy® KickStart Book – *TAROT TWIST* - will provide you many innovative Spreads for responding to people's questions as you gain more experience. You can start straight out of the box with the two example spreads we have given at the end of this present book.

We have concluded each card with an "Oracular Title". These are the titles of the cards that have arisen from readers suggestions when they have linked the card to some other concept or metaphor – such as a child on a Carousel (6 of Wands). These titles provide slightly enigmatic yet obvious examples of the cards theme in action and are invaluable for understanding the cards deeper meanings and application in a reading. We have also given an oracular title for the card if it is flipped (reversed).

These keywords and themes have arisen by asking experienced readers themselves to derive meaning from the scenes on the cards themselves, hence these are *intuited* meanings based on the readers own knowledge and experience. You may compare these "in the field" meanings with the various Kabbalistic, Numerological, Esoteric and Book/Individual meanings to see how they compare and contrast – and in doing so, distil further your own personal interpretation of each card.

Of course, there is no singular meaning of any card, yet each one is different to another – so in a sense the "meaning" of a card becomes a *strange attractor*, something to which every interpretation approaches, but never attains. This is part of the power of Tarot as a tool – the symbols on each card are *multivalent*, having many meanings, which gives rise to a complex constellation of possible interpretations. This makes it possible to apply it to any context, and position, any spread and any question.

We have demonstrated the application of the keywords and phrases in this Tarosophy® Kickstart Reference Book in two sample readings/spreads at the conclusion of the book.

The Suits

Pentacles:	Resources
Swords:	Expectations
Cups:	Imagination
Wands:	Ambition

The Minors

Ace:	Seed
Two:	Organization
Three:	Activation
Four:	Application
Five:	Boundary
Six:	Utilization
Seven:	Reorganization
Eight:	Direction
Nine:	Rest
Ten:	Return

The Court Cards

Page: Channeling

Knight: Responding

Queen: Connecting

King: Demonstrating

Using the Reference Tables to Generate Meanings

Putting the Unconscious Keywords together produces, for example:

Four of Swords: The Application of Expectations.

The keyword generated for this card by readers was "Hiding". We see this, in the light of the standard meanings of the card, as applying thoughts and ideas either in an obvious way or a cunning fashion. Thus, the oracular titles of *A Museum where the Labels are Misleading* and the Flip Title, *Children Playing Hide and Seek*.

The Theme/Framework that supports these concepts is that of *Reality*. This provides a meta-frame for the card and its interpretation in any context.

When you look at a card such as found in the Waite-Smith Tarot, which shows a Knight in Armor in repose in a Chapel, you can read this as a "reality check" in contemporary terms instead of a "retreat" or "rest from strife" as given in many books. In this "reality check" it is a time to apply what you expected to what has happened so far. Perhaps the labels you have given things is not what they actually are – just like in the oracular title.

The use of these keywords and concepts gives the new Reader a much more contemporary and applicable set of ideas with which to interpret the cards. It also gives experienced readers a fresh set of ideas to compare to their own existing concepts.

Key Theme for Pentacles: RESOURCES

Ace of Pentacles: The Seed of Resource

Upright: **Wealth**

What you say: "This card promises resources and wealth ahead from this seed"

Reversed: **Ruin**

What you say: "This card reversed indicates a collapse of everything being built"

Theme/Framework: Resources

Oracular Title: A Wealthy Man In His Garden

Flip Title: A Man Unable to Pay His Debts

2 of Pentacles: The Organisation of Resource

Upright: **Organization**

What you say: "With this card you must organize yourself and your resources"

Reversed: **Disorganization**

What you say: "This card symbolizes a lack of balance"

Theme/Framework: Order

Oracular Title: A Ship Cresting the Waves of the Sea

Flip Title: A Sailing Crew who are Unfamiliar to Each Other

3 of Pentacles: The Activating of Resource

Upright: **Loyalty**

What you say: "This card shows someone who is committed"

Reversed: **Resigning**

What you say: "This card flipped indicates someone who gives up"

Theme/Framework: Planning

Oracular Title: A Woman Working at Her Desk

Flip Title: A Woman Handing in Her Notice

4 of Pentacles: The Application of Resource

Upright: **Selfishness**

What you say: "In the appearance of this card, we see a selfish nature"

Reversed: **Generosity**

What you say: "This card upside down shows a time to be generous"

Theme/Framework: Attachment

Oracular Title: Four Coins Thrown Into A Well

Flip Title: A Party Which Has Got Out of Hand

5 of Pentacles: The Boundary of Resource

Upright: **Loss**

What you say: "The appearance of this card shows a loss"

Reversed: **Fulfilled Expectations**

What you say: "In this card reversed your expectations will be met"

Theme/Framework: Competition

Oracular Title: A Lost Lottery Ticket

Flip Title: A Child Wins on a Sideshow Competition

6 of Pentacles: The Use of Resource

Upright: **Resources**

What you say: "This card indicates you gain the resources you require"

Reversed: **Lack of Resource**

What you say: "When this card is upside-down it shows that you will not have the resources you require"

Theme/Framework: Environment

Oracular Title: A Landscape Garden which is Well-Maintained

Flip Title: Six People Lost in an Overgrown Garden

7 of Pentacles: The Reorganisation of Resource

Upright: **Cultivation**

What you say: "This card demonstrates that what you reap, you sow"

Reversed: **Barrenness**

What you say: "When this card appears reversed, there will be no fruit to your labors"

Theme/Framework: Response

Oracular Title: A Flowering Bush Which has been Well-Tended

Flip Title: A Boy Waiting in an Empty Space

8 of Pentacles: The Direction of Resource

Upright: **Self-Confidence**

What you say: "When this card turns up it shows you should have the confidence in your own abilities"

Reversed: **Self-Doubt**

What you say: "This card, when reversed, suggests self-doubt"

Theme/Framework: Assessment

Oracular Title: A Market Place full of Jewels

Flip Title: A Man Working in an Empty Shop

9 of Pentacles: The Resting of Resource

Upright: **Selfishness**

What you say: "This card signifies holding on to things"

Reversed: **Sharing**

What you say: "This card (reversed) signifies letting go of things"

Theme/Framework: Possession

Oracular Title: A bird of prey fastened to the wrist

Flip Title: A bird flying free to return

10 of Pentacles: The Return of Resource

Upright: **Good Returns**

What you say: "This card shows that all will be well with the matter"

Reversed: **Lack of Return**

What you say: "When this card is flipped, it shows a lack of return for the work you have put in"

Theme/Framework: Return

Oracular Title: A Rich Man in His Family Manor

Flip Title: A Family in Hard Times

Page of Pentacles: Resource Channelling

Upright: **Starting Work**

What you say: "This card shows a channeling to your resources"

Reversed: **Waste**

What you say: "When reversed, this card indicates you may have lost a grip on your resources"

Theme/Framework: Control

Oracular Title: A Young Person Holding a Ball

Flip Title: Children Looking for a Lost Penny

Knight of Pentacles: Resource Responding

Upright: **Capability**

What you say: "This figure shows that you are capable and able to meet your goal so long as you maintain focus"

Reversed: **Incapability**

What you say: "When upside-down, this figure shows that you are easily distracted from your goals"

Theme/Framework: Ability

Oracular Title: A Knight in Armor Arrives at the Tournament.

Flip Title: A Broken Shell Lies on a Vast Beach

Queen of Pentacles: Resource Connecting

Upright: **Nurturing**

What you say: "With the Queen of Pentacles, you are able to nurture your state and environment over time"

Reversed: **Neglecting**

What you say: "You are neglecting what can be grown"

Theme/Framework: Care

Oracular Title: The Sun and Rain in a Shady Place

Flip Title: An Old Garden Gate Swinging Open in the Wind

King of Pentacles: Resource Demonstrating

Upright: **Obviousness**

What you say: "What you see is what you get"

Reversed: **Hiding**

What you say: "There are things you need which are being hidden"

Theme/Framework: Discovery

Oracular Title: On A Plate There is Good Food

Flip Title: A Man At A Costume Party

Key Theme for Swords: EXPECTATIONS

Ace of Swords: The Seed of Expectation

Upright: **Movement**

What you say: "With the powerful Ace of Swords, things get moving!"

Reversed: **Fixation**

What you say: "Things are fixed when the Ace of Swords is reversed."

Theme/Framework: Expectation

Oracular Title: Light Streaming Through an Open Library Window.

Flip Title: A Sealed Envelope Passed From Hand to Hand.

2 of Swords: The Organisation of Expectation

Upright: **Confusion**

What you say: "In this symbol we see clearly the confusion of the mind"

Reversed: **Clarity**

What you say: "When reversed, the Two of Swords shows immediate decision being called into action"

Theme/Framework: Organization

Oracular Title: Many Papers Thrown to the Wind.

Flip Title: A Voice Raised Above the Crowd.

3 of Swords: The Activation of Expectation

Upright: **Disappointment**

What you say: "With this card we see that you will be disappointed in your expectations, calling those expectations into question."

Reversed: **Expansion**

What you say: "Reversed, this card means expansion of those things you expect."

Theme/Framework: Concern

Oracular Title: A Rain that Comes At The Wrong Time.

Flip Title: People Making Space for Someone on a Crowded Train.

4 of Swords: The Application of Expectation

Upright: **Hiding**

What you say: "You are hiding from the facts, perhaps not seeing the obvious, which is causing you disturbance."

Reversed: **Truth**

What you say: "You must face the facts as they are, not what you want them to be"

Theme/Framework: Reality

Oracular Title: A Museum where the Labels are Misleading.

Flip Title: Children Playing Hide and Seek.

5 of Swords: The Boundary of Expectation

Upright: **Defeat**

What you say: "You may exceed yourself and meet defeat on this present course of thinking."

Reversed: **Winning**

What you say: "When this card is upside-down, it denotes that you will win in your decision-making."

Theme/Framework: Appreciation

Oracular Title: A Woman Turning Away from Her Reflection.

Flip Title: A Carpenter Arrives with His Toolkit.

6 of Swords: The Utilization of Expectation

Upright: **Holiday**

What you say: "You can see in this card a suggestion that you know when to quit when you are ahead and take your winnings."

Reversed: **Work**

What you say: "This card reversed means that you have to work hard to get where you are thinking you should be."

Theme/Framework: Responsibility

Oracular Title: A Family on the Ferry.

Flip Title: A Man Pushing a Broken-Down Vehicle.

7 of Swords: The Reorganization of Expectation

Upright: **Trespass**

What you say: "In this card, we see in the situation for which we are reading some indication of deceit – someone is breaking the agreement."

Reversed: **Integrity**

What you say: "When this card is reversed, we know that all is being honestly presented."

Theme/Framework: Exchange

Oracular Title: A Sign Reading Don't Walk on the Grass.

Flip Title: A Man Borrowing Books from a Library.

8 of Swords: The Direction of Expectation

Upright: **Trust**

What you say: "Have faith in the direction in which things are progressing."

Reversed: **Mistrust**

What you say: "Don't believe how things are going – doubt may uncover problems not yet apparent."

Theme/Framework: Knowledge

Oracular Title: A Mail Train on the Tracks.

Flip Title: A Newspaper full of Propaganda.

9 of Swords: The Rest of Expectation

Upright: **Pessimism**

What you say: "You cannot see in the gloom – doubt of thought makes you feel emotionally hopeless"

Reversed: **Optimism**

What you say: "Whilst it is great to think positively, this card reversed shows honest thinking leading to joy."

Theme/Framework: Expression

Oracular Title: A Nursery at Night-time, A Dark Cradle.

Flip Title: A Schoolchild Greets the Summer Holidays.

10 of Swords: The Return of Expectation

Upright: **Distress**

What you say: "This foreboding card warns of the stress of being divided in mind about a matter."

Reversed: **Delight**

What you say: "Reversed, this particular card shows delight and cause for celebration that a close shave has been avoided."

Theme/Framework: Division

Oracular Title: Rain Falling on a Broken Mirror.

Flip Title: A Group Dancing with Tambourines.

Page of Swords: Expectation Channeling

Upright: **Obedience**

What you say: "The Page of Swords indicates that the energy which must be applied should follow the rules laid down for the particular game."

Reversed: **Disobedience**

What you say: "It is time to break some rules!"

Theme/Framework: Law

Oracular Title: A Windmill Turning in a Good Wind.

Flip Title: Children Throwing Stones at Windows.

Knight of Swords: Expectation Responding

Upright: **Pursuit**

What you say: "In this card we clearly see the energy that you must bring to bear – pursuing what it is that you believe in."

Reversed: **Retreat**

What you say: "It is time to make an orderly retreat from the situation; it is suggested by this card."

Theme/Framework: Conflict

Oracular Title: A Man in a Vehicle Chases the Storm.

Flip Title: A Rabbit Takes Shelter in the Rain.

Queen of Swords: Expectation Connecting

Upright: **Acknowledgement**

What you say: "The Queen of Swords is ruthless but fair in giving her advice in a question. She shows here that your worth will be recognized."

Reversed: **Refusing**

What you say: "The Queen of Swords is a little heartless I am afraid, and here shows when she is reversed that there will be a refusal to your intentions. It may even be 'Off With Your Head' so hold on tight."

Theme/Framework: Permission

Oracular Title: A Girl Dressed for Her Debutante Ball.

Flip Title: A Man Misses his Connecting Flight.

King of Swords: Expectation Demonstrating

Upright: **Deliberation**

What you say: "The King of Swords is at the top of his game and counsels that you take time to deliberate your options before acting."

Reversed: **Thoughtlessness**

What you say: "The King of Swords is least happy upside-down, when confusion or other factors can lead to thoughtlessness. Take a moment to consider the situation."

Theme/Framework: Thought

Oracular Title: A Judge Waiting on the Jury to Speak.

Flip Title: A Deck of Cards Scattered to the Winds.

Key Theme for Cups: IMAGINATION

Ace of Cups: The Seed of Imagination

Upright: **Motion**

What you say: "Things are moving freely in this card, as in life. Fulfillment. Go with the flow."

Reversed: **Stagnancy**

What you say: "The Ace of Cups reversed shows a stagnant situation, often emotional, which will inevitably drain you. There is nothing new here."

Theme/Framework: Imagination

Oracular Title: An Artist with A Peacock Feather in their Hand.

Flip Title: A Large Dam in a Distant Place.

2 of Cups: The Organisation of Imagination

Upright: **Trust**

What you say: "In this well-aspected image, we see the idea of total trust being given and received."

Reversed: **Singleness**

What you say: "Reversed, this card, the Two of Cups, perhaps tells us that you must have a singular perspective on this matter, and go it alone."

Theme/Framework: Organization

Oracular Title: A Contract on A Well-Worn Desk.

Flip Title: A Horse Walking Steadily Across an Empty Desert.

3 of Cups: The Activation of Imagination

Upright: **Harmony**

What you say: "A time of contentment is predicted by this card. You will be satisfied by what follows."

Reversed: **Disharmony**

What you say: "Your imagination can create scenes which can make you jealous or envious. Do not punish yourself with these images."

Theme/Framework: Consideration

Oracular Title: Three Cats Sleeping In a Summer Yard.

Flip Title: A Face Looking in Through a Window.

4 of Cups: The Application of Imagination

Upright: **Distraction**

What you say: "It is already too late when you are over-striving. The answer was right where you started."

Reversed: **Calling**

What you say: "Reversed, this card shows that a calling is present — tranquility is required to hear this calling. Quiet down now."

Theme/Framework: Vocation

Oracular Title: A Stained Glass Window Reflecting on a Floor.

Flip Title: A Salmon Swimming Up-River.

5 of Cups: The Boundary of Imagination

Upright: **Guilt**

What you say: "You feel sorrow that you have not lived up to your own image of yourself."

Reversed: **Innocence**

What you say: "You will reach your goal so long as you remain pure to the task you set yourself in your heart."

Theme/Framework: Acceptance

Oracular Title: A Broken Drum Discarded underneath a Christmas Tree.

Flip Title: A Mountain Stream Reflecting Sunlight.

6 of Cups: The Utilization of Imagination

Upright: **Immaturity**

What you say: "If you heed the Six of Cups, you will take advice to grow up and leave the childish attractions."

Reversed: **Maturity**

What you say: "This card flipped indicates a maturity and presence of heart to know how this situation plays out."

Theme/Framework: Age

Oracular Title: A Rocket Ship Leaves the Earth.

Flip Title: A Clock in the Kings Hall Striking Noon.

7 of Cups: The Reorganisation of Imagination

Upright: **Release**

What you say: "This interesting card, full of symbols, shows that it is timely to release your emotions despite what shadows they may make."

Reversed: **Collecting**

What you say: "When this card shows up in a reading flipped upside-down, it's telling us that you should be collecting your thoughts, not being overshadowed by them, OK?"

Theme/Framework: Acquisition

Oracular Title: The Signing of Deeds to a New House.

Flip Title: A Childs Stamp Collection in an Attic.

8 of Cups: The Direction of Imagination

Upright: **Attending**

What you say: "Whilst this card may show a dismal scene, it can be read as a calling to attend to one's own needs or the needs of others."

Reversed: **Absence**

What you say: "This card reversed is a flip in that it denotes absence – perhaps one which cannot be avoided. Oftentimes, this absence is an opportunity for you to find the space you need."

Theme/Framework: Place

Oracular Title: A Dog At His Masters Feet.

Flip Title: An Empty Space on a Park Bench.

9 of Cups: The Rest of Imagination

Upright: **Fulfillment**

What you say: "This card is perhaps the happiest card to receive in that it shows that you receive the fruits of your labours in good time."

Reversed: **Disappointment**

What you say: "Your labours will amount to nothing by the appearance of this card in a reversed position. You should prepare to reconsider."

Theme/Framework: Accounting

Oracular Title: A Feast at Harvest Time.

Flip Title: A Cupboard Full of Shoes with One Missing.

10 of Cups: The Return of Imagination

Upright: **Ecstasy**

What you say: "A beautiful card which shows a heavenly situation, past or outcome for your situation."

Reversed: **Heartache**

What you say: "This usually bright card in a reversed position does tend to show heartache and emotional poverty."

Theme/Framework: Values

Oracular Title: A Phoenix in a Story Book.

Flip Title: A Burnt Catherine Wheel After the Firework Party.

Upright: **Sophistication**

What you say: "With this Court Card, the Page of Cups, we can read that this situation requires a careful and elegant approach, almost bordering on performance!"

Reversed: **Primitive**

What you say: "It's time to get real and just burst through the complexities by returning to basics."

Theme/Framework: Culture

Oracular Title: A Fountain Cascading in a Stately Home.

Flip Title: A Dripping Tap in a Silent Room.

Knight of Cups: Imagination Responding

Upright: **Exhibition**

What you say: "You see in this card that – much like the character shown – you are being advised to strut your stuff!"

Reversed: **Recluse**

What you say: "In this card, with this character, reversed, you are being made aware that you are trying too hard to impress. Time to return to your own space for a while."

Theme/Framework: Presentation

Oracular Title: An Artist at a Gallery Exhibiting Paintings of Peacocks.

Flip Title: Sunflowers Wilting During a Heatwave

Queen of Cups: Imagination Connecting

Upright: **Affection**

What you say: "The Queen of Cups shows that we must connect to others in a truly affectionate manner."

Reversed: **Conceit**

What you say: "Hmmmm …. Someone has too high an opinion of themselves!"

Theme/Framework: Sensitivity

Oracular Title: A Paper-Chain Cut Out in the Shape of Hearts.

Flip Title: A Carnival Show House of Mirrors.

King of Cups: Imagination Demonstrating

Upright: **Recognition**

What you say: "The King of Cups shows that this time is one where you must recognize yourself (or others) for their feelings."

Reversed: **Forgetfulness**

What you say: "When flipped, the King of Cups counsels forgetting as the best approach in this situation, no matter how hard that may be."

Theme/Framework: Memory

Oracular Title: A Father Showing His Son How to Swim.

Flip Title: Icicles Melting in a Spring Thaw.

Key Theme for Wands: AMBITION

Ace of Wands: The Seed of Ambition

Upright: **Advancement**

What you say: "The powerful Ace of Wands brings growth, gain, and the promise of steady progress."

Reversed: **Interruption**

What you say: "Reversed, this powerful card, the Ace of Wands, brings a break to your plans."

Theme/Framework: Ambition

Oracular Title: A Green Flag Flying in a High Breeze.

Flip Title: A Broken Stick on a Pavement.

2 of Wands: The Organisation of Ambition

Upright: **Planning**

What you say: "The Two of Wands here shows that your aims need structure and thought for your goal before it is too late."

Reversed: **Ignoring**

What you say: "Whilst you go forwards, it is never too late to look around and ensure you have everything you need."

Theme/Framework: Organization

Oracular Title: An Empty Suitcase on a Bed Surrounded by Clothes.

Flip Title: A Person Turning Away From A Friend Calling Them.

3 of Wands: The Activation of Ambition

Upright: **Building**

What you say: "When this card appears, it signifies a time of building and growth in your plans."

Reversed: **Dismantling**

What you say: "When this card appears reversed, it is time to take apart your work so far and look to start again."

Theme/Framework: Creation

Oracular Title: An Artists Palette in an Empty Church.

Flip Title: Autumn Leaves in a Quiet Park.

4 of Wands: The Application of Ambition

Upright: **Welcoming, appropriate response**

What you say: "This card means you get an appropriate response"

Reversed: **Loss, Exile**

What you say: "This card (reversed) means you are pushed out"

Theme/Framework: Sympathy

Oracular Title: An Appropriate Greeting from a Group of People

Flip Title: An Inappropriate Greeting

5 of Wands: The Boundary of Ambition

Upright: **Disconnection**

What you say: "It is time to disconnect from those around you, or to take action with those who are hindering your plans. A big change is required."

Reversed: **Connection**

What you say: "This card when flipped may indicate that you are ready to communicate and collaborate with another. This will further your plans."

Theme/Framework: Society

Oracular Title: A Broken Telegraph Wire in a Time of War.

Flip Title: Architects Around a Table Discussing Their Drawing Whilst the Building Goes on Outside the Window.

6 of Wands: The Utilization of Ambition

Upright: **Amusement**

What you say: "This card, whilst appearing to denote celebration, offers advice that one should not be easily amused lest the joke be played on you."

Reversed: **Weariness**

What you say: "It is time to take a well-earned rest from the effort you have already extended. It is deserved."

Theme/Framework: Entertainment

Oracular Title: A Masqued Party Applauding.

Flip Title: A Child Riding on a Carousel.

7 of Wands: The Reorganization of Ambition

Upright: **Exposure**

What you say: "It is time to make your plans known!"

Reversed: **Concealment**

What you say: "It is time to hide what you are doing until you are fully ready to reveal it."

Theme/Framework: Communication

Oracular Title: Soldiers Radio In Their Position.

Flip Title: An Innocent Prisoner Goes into Hiding.

8 of Wands: The Direction of Ambition

Upright: **Management**

What you say: "It is time to take a grip of everything involved in this situation."

Reversed: **Misdirection**

What you say: "You may feel as if nothing is going your way, and there is some possibility of willful steering of you by another."

Theme/Framework: Observation

Oracular Title: A Perfect Flight of Geese at the Right Time of Year.

Flip Title: A Magician Performing a Magical Trick.

9 of Wands: The Rest of Ambition

Upright: **Care**

What you say: "This card signifies that you must exercise caution in this matter."

Reversed: **Approachability**

What you say: "You may allow others to get close to you in this matter, when this card is showing upside-down."

Theme/Framework: Review

Oracular Title: A Warden Making the Prison Rounds.

Flip Title: A Woman Meeting a Good Friend at a Train Station.

10 of Wands: The Return of Ambition

Upright: **Work**

What you say: "In this card, the Ten of Wands, we see that you are being required to work to consolidate your vision."

Reversed: **Sloth**

What you say: "When reversed, the Ten of Wands shows that you are letting things decay by laziness."

Theme/Framework: Capability

Oracular Title: Bees Working in a Hive on a Sunny Day.

Flip Title: A Rusting Spade Abandoned in the Rain.

Page of Wands: Ambition Channelling

Upright: **Entrance**

What you say: "This card, the Page of Wands, clearly means that you are about to enter into a new phase of your lifestyle."

Reversed: **Retirement**

What you say: "When flipped, the Page here suggests it is time to take an early retirement from whatever you are struggling with."

Theme/Framework: Engagement

Oracular Title: A Ship is Launched by the Latest Celebrity.

Flip Title: Miners Leave the Coal Mine for the Last Time.

Knight of Wands: Ambition Responding

Upright: **Advancement**

What you say: "The Knight of Wands shows here that your advancement is reasonably assured."

Reversed: **Hesitation**

What you say: "Caution is the watchword for when the Knight of Swords appears in a flipped position. He who hesitates is not always lost."

Theme/Framework: Positioning.

Oracular Title: Knights Approach the Chapel of the Grail.

Flip Title: A Red Key Adorned with Petals Does Not Unlock the Gate.

Upright: **Independence**

What you say: "When connected to your heart's ambitions, this card carries the meaning of true independence and self-will."

Reversed: **Dependence**

What you say: "This card is not happy reversed and tells us that you should not be so reliant on others for your own goals."

Theme/Framework: Belonging

Oracular Title: A Movie Star Makes Her Entrance

Flip Title: A Servant Lights the Fire for His Master.

King of Wands: Ambition Demonstrating

Upright: **Authenticity**

What you say: "The King of Wands is a powerful card which shows that true honesty leads to authenticity and power."

Reversed: **Falseness**

What you say: "The King of Wands flipped gives the advice that you should 'to your own self be true'."

Theme/Framework: Identity

Oracular Title: The Sun Shines Down on a Clock Tower at Noon.

Flip Title: Wax Fruit in a Theatre Production.

In the creation of these keywords, we noticed some incredible unconscious patterns in the ideas which were provided by many Tarot readers. You will notice that the central theme which we found in the majority of each suit was most evident in the Ace of the Suit.

The Ace of the Suit provides the seed concept which grows into the remaining cards of the suit. We have reflected this by giving the theme of the Ace of each Suit the identical theme of the Suit.

The Two of Pentacles reflected strongly the nature of the "Two" in all Suits, i.e. organization. This we take to indicate that the Pentacles manifest the processes of the other Suits. The Pentacles are the making real of the other ideas found throughout the deck. When a Pentacle is present, things will be happening in the noticeable world of events!

You will also notice the Twos are Organizers and the Sevens are Reorganizers. You may compare the Twos and Sevens of each Suit and see if this fits for your deck and appreciation of that deck.

Threes and Fours are activating and applying cards, they seem close together but the Three is like the motor running after ignition and the Four the pedal going down in the vehicle to make it move!

The Fives represent the transition boundary of the theme of the Suit. They are difficult only when this transition is resisted. These Fives in each Suit are truly the "Calling Cards".

We also found the Sixes reflecting the theme of their Suit. This is very appropriate in Kabbalah, where each Tree of Life in the "four worlds" grows out of the sixth Sephiroth of each Tree. When a Six is present, we see a "flip" in the energy of the situation – things are being taken to another level when these cards appear.

The Eights are directive cards, which can particularly be seen in the Suit of Wands, Ambition. The Nines represent the Resting of the theme, its final phase until the Ten shows it returning to the start of the Cycle.

Thus, Ambition when fulfilled (9 of Wands) is always incomplete until the Return to the original impulse of the activity (10 of Wands) leads to completion and frees a new beginning (Ace of Wands).

The Alchemical Stages and the Hero's Journey might be better seen in the progression of the Ace to 10 of each Suit than the Majors.

You may discover other patterns and significance in the Oracular Titles of these cards, which might be considered a dream or racial-unconscious version of the visible cards themselves.

Making A Card Fit

No matter what card arrives in which position of a spread, or in answer to a general question, an experienced reader is able to interpret its meaning. However, when we start from basic keywords and concepts, this can often be difficult for those new to Tarot. How does one apply a card whose word is "trespass" to a question about one's college exam?

In NLP, we use a method called "chunking" which describes levels of detail applied to thinking. A model of lateral thinking shows how people chunk in a particular "strategy" (which is unconscious) to solve problems in a creative way. We have applied this model to produce a KickStart version of "making a card fit" as follows.

Example: 3 of Wands in the "past" position of a spread where the question was about a relationship. This card has the keyword of **building** and the title 'Activation of Ambition'. To make this fit, we map the context (or metaphor) in which building makes sense to the context of the question – the relationship. So "building" takes place in a context of 'building a house'. We then compare building a house to a relationship. Obviously, the building comes early in the process, as it would do in the relationship – the house is also about security. So, we then apply this to a relationship, perhaps seeing that the relationship was "cemented" in the past, based on the persons high ideals for the union. Those "foundations" are now in the past denoting the relationship – like the building – has moved on.

Example: 6 of Wands in the "Advice" position of a particular spread. This card has the keyword of **Weariness**. This is part of the context of 'entertainment' so we would fit it into the reading by saying the Querent is advised not to treat the situation as a game, otherwise they will tire of it.

We believe that by using the "flip" method to derive these keywords they will prove universal. However, insight always comes by working with the cards themselves in a range of questions – go practice!

The Keywords for the Majors are taken from the "Never" exercise in *Tarosophy®* where these concepts were generated from many hundreds of entries by Tarot readers. They are explored further in *Tarosophy®*. The Majors do not have Oracular Titles other than their own title and no themes as they are already images of archetypes.

A very simple reversal/flip is given here for the Majors which is suitable for your first practice readings – for more elegant reversal methods please consult Mary K. Greer's *Complete Tarot Reversals*.

I: Magician

Upright: **Success**

What you say: "The Magician brings success and resource to your endeavors."

Reversed: **Failure**

What you say: "The reversed Magician indicates you do not have the required resources for what you wish to perform."

II: High Priestess

Upright: **Revelation**

What you say: "The High Priestess will reveal what is hidden."

Reversed: **Secrecy**

What you say: "When reversed, the High Priestess tells us that something is being concealed."

III: Empress

Upright: **Cultivation**

What you say: "The Empress brings gradual growth to your life."

Reversed: **Harm**

What you say: "The reversed Empress warns that harm may come about in your intended actions."

IV: Emperor

Upright: **Endurance**

What you say: "The Emperor signifies power and endurance to your situation."

Reversed: **Instability**

What you say: "When reversed, the Emperor can show the instability of the situation is important."

V: Hierophant

Upright: **Teaching**

What you say: "When the Hierophant appears, he says that we must teach."

Reversed: **Learning**

What you say: "When the Hierophant is reversed, we are being told to learn."

VI: Lovers

Upright: **Union**

What you say: "The Lovers brings all things together."

Reversed: **Separation**

What you say: "The Lovers flipped brings separation."

VII: Chariot

Upright: **Momentum**

What you say: "The Chariot brings great forward energy to the event."

Reversed: **Stop**

What you say: "When reversed, the Chariot brings a full halt to your energies and projects."

VIII: Strength

Upright: **Action**

What you say: "'Take action' is the message that Strength brings in a reading."

Reversed: **Rest**

What you say: "When reversed, the Strength card shows a rest is called for to establish a better relationship to your life."

IX: Hermit

Upright: **Solitude**

What you say: "The Hermit signifies simply solitude. Time to be by yourself."

Reversed: **Companionship**

What you say: "The exact opposite of being a Hermit is to seek out companionship, which is the message of this card when flipped."

X: Wheel

Upright: **Movement**

What you say: "The Wheel means that everything that happens is connected and moves the situation forwards."

Reversed: **Pause**

What you say: "When reversed, the Wheel shows we must take a pause and regain the centre."

XI: Justice

Upright: **Accuracy**

What you say: "This card, Justice, shows that there is a fair response to the situation. You reap what you sow."

Reversed: **Mistake**

What you say: "When upside-down, Justice can mean a mistake is being made."

XII: Hanged Man

Upright: **Surrender**

What you say: "Time to let go and surrender to your highest principles."

Reversed: **Struggle**

What you say: "Time to struggle to ensure your viewpoint is seen."

XIII: Death

Upright: **Life**

What you say: "The Death card, strangely, shows transformation and new life in your situation."

Reversed: **Stagnation**

What you say: "Here, reversed, is the Death card, showing that everything will stagnate and rot in this position. Not a happy card."

XIV: Temperance

Upright: **Assessment**

What you say: "When the Temperance card appears, it suggests we assess the situation in a balanced manner."

Reversed: **Over-Compensation**

What you say: "Reversed, Temperance can show that we are out of balance and over-reacting to the situation."

XV: Devil

Upright: **Withholding**

What you say: "The Devil card in this reading means that not all has been released – something is being withheld."

Reversed: **Liberation**

What you say: "The Devil, when flipped, is a card of release and liberation. Good times!"

XVI: Blasted Tower

Upright: **Acceleration**

What you say: "The Tower never asks – it just happens. An acceleration of events will bring things to a sudden change."

Reversed: **Fall**

What you say: "When reversed, the Tower shows things crashing down in slow-motion. Not a great card."

XVII: Star

Upright: **Enlightenment**

What you say: "The beautiful Star card symbolizes the light of vision leading you to a better future."

Reversed: **Darkness**

What you say: "When the Star is reversed, you must trust your instincts as things otherwise are unclear and unlit."

XVIII: Moon

Upright: **Ignorance**

What you say: "The Moon card in your reading shows us that some things are unknown, and we must learn more to progress."

Reversed: **Knowledge**

What you say: "When upside-down, the Moon indicates knowledge. It appears that we know everything we need to know about this question."

XIX: Sun

Upright: **Demonstration**

What you say: "The Sun shines equally on everything, meaning that this part of your reading is bright and obvious. Good news!"

Reversed: **Concealment**

What you say: "Like the Sun behind clouds, when this card is reversed, it means that things are being hidden at this time."

XX: Last Judgment

Upright: **Awakening**

What you say: "The Last Judgment card is a significant card in a reading in that it shows us which part of your life needs awakening."

Reversed: **Sleep**

What you say: "When reversed, this card means that you must let sleeping dogs lie."

Upright: **Beginning**

What you say: "The World brings new beginnings and the dance of Life itself. A powerful and comprehensive card to empower your life."

Reversed: **Ending**

What you say: "When reversed, the World maintains much of the same meaning, only signifying somewhat more of the ending of the old life prior to the beginning of the new."

0: Fool

Upright: **Frivolity**

What you say: "Take a light-hearted leap into the unknown, for you are free!"

Reversed: **Seriousness**

What you say: "The Fool doesn't stay flipped for long! Before you know it, you'll be laughing about this situation!"

In this simple spread, suitable for beginner practice, we shuffle and take three cards out of the deck to create a story of three parts: past, present and future.

The question asked is:

"What can the Tarot tell me about the situation with my neighbors?"

The Three cards selected from the top of the shuffled deck are:

Past: Temperance (XIV) Reversed

Present: Knight of Wands

Future: The Magician (I)

We then consult the appropriate entries in this Kickstart Guide to produce the following reading:

"In the past" … "Reversed, Temperance can show that we are out of balance and over-reacting to the situation."

"In the present" … "The Knight of Wands shows here that your advancement is reasonably assured."

"In the future" … "The Magician brings success and resource to your endeavors."

This would seem to indicate that the Querent (asking the question) has had a bad experience in the past regarding neighbors, which is being brought into the present moment. However, this experience has actually given them all the knowledge and resources they need to deal with the present situation to a successful conclusion. A positive reading!

In this practical spread, we look to get the best out of a situation based upon the four elements + spirit, arranged on a Pentagram:

1. **Earth** – the Practical

2. **Air** – the Mental

3. **Water** – the Emotional

4. **Fire** – the Magical/Transformative

5. **Spirit** – the Spiritual

So, the question asked might be, "What do I need to know to get the best out of my new relationship?"

The Five Cards pulled might be:

1. Practical – 8 of Swords (reversed)
2. Mental – Knight of Swords (reversed)
3. Emotional – 7 of Swords
4. Magical – Empress (III)
5. Spiritual – King of Swords

Taking the relevant sections of this KickStart Guide, we can weave an interpretation as follows:

> "On the practical level of this new relationship, don't believe how things are going – doubt may uncover problems not yet apparent. Your ideas may be getting the best of you - it is time to make an orderly retreat from the situation; it is suggested by this card.
>
> Regarding the spiritual aspects of the new relationship, The King of Swords is at the top of his game and counsels that you take time to deliberate your options before acting. Again, this is a card of caution.
>
> On the other side of the Pentagram, we see in the Seven of Swords, we see in the situation for which we are reading some indication of deceit – someone is breaking the agreement.
>
> From a magical perspective, in terms of how this will transform you, the Empress brings gradual growth to your life."

Obviously, this reading – being mainly of Swords and cards of caution and concern, counsels the Querent to think before acting in the new relationship. You can then look back over the Keywords, Themes and even the Oracular Titles to clarify further aspects of this reading.

We trust you will find many weeks and months of discovery with your deck and this first Tarosophy® KickStart Guide. It has been a pleasure to produce it and play with the ideas to provide a fresh new look at Tarot.

It is not intended to be a definitive guide to Tarot keywords or concepts - far from it! We have provided two books in the Reading List for you to discover how many different ways there are of conceptualizing and describing all 78 cards in a Tarot deck!

This Guide is merely an introduction to fast-track you into reading so you can begin to develop more quickly than you might have thought possible. You can then move onto developing spreads through the next book, Tarot Twist, and beyond!

We have also provided in the final section a list of reading materials and website resources to discover more in the absolute best of Tarot and Tarosophy®.

Titles in this innovative series of Tarosophy® KickStart Guides.

Volume I.

Book I: *Tarot Flip* - Reading Tarot Straight from the Box
Book II: *Tarot Twist* - Finding a Spread for Every Question
Book III: *Tarot Inspire* – Explore your Spiritual Life with Tarot

Volume II.

Book I: *Tarot Switch* – Use Magical Tarot methods to change your Life
Book II: *Tarot Uplift* – Experience Tarot and Kabbalah for Initiation
Book III: *Tarot Divine* - Encounter the Mystical Teachings of Tarot

Further Reading

The following titles have been chosen specifically to provide a comprehensive guide to keywords and reversals to further your exploration and enjoyment of your Tarot reading.

Tarosophy, Marcus Katz (Keswick: Forge Press, 2016)

Tarot Reversals, Mary K. Greer (St. Paul: Llewellyn, 2004)

The Definitive Tarot (also pub. as *Tarot Bible)*, Bill Butler (London: Rider & Co, 1975)

Tarot Dictionary & Compendium, Jana Riley (York Beach: Samuel Weiser, Inc., 1995)

Tarot 101, Kim Huggens (Woodbury: Llewellyn, 2010)

Tarot for Beginners, Barbara Moore (Woodbury: Llewellyn, 2010)

Websites & Resources

Tarot Association: http://www.tarotprofessionals.com

Tarot Professionals Facebook Group

http://www.facebook.com/groups/tarotprofessionals

Free Tarot Card Meanings & Spreads

http://www.mytarotcardmeanings.com